NATURE'S MYSTERIES

HOW SPIDERS
MAKE THEIR WEBS

Jill Bailey

BENCHMARK BOOKS

MARSHALL CAVENDISH
NEW YORK

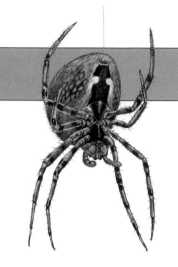

Benchmark Books
Marshall Cavendish Corporation
99 White Plains Road
Tarrytown, New York 10591-9001

©Marshall Cavendish Corporation, 1997

Series created by The Creative Publishing Company

Library of Congress Cataloging-in-Publication Data
Bailey, Jill.
    How spiders make their webs / Jill Bailey.
       p.   cm. -- (Nature's mysteries)
    Includes bibliographical references and index.
    Summary: Describes different kinds of spiders, the types of webs
they spin, and the various purposes these webs serve.
    ISBN 0-7614-0456-2 (lib. bdg.)
    1. Spider webs--Juvenile literature.   2. Spiders--Juvenile
literature. [1. Spiders. 2. Spider webs.]   I. Title.
II. Series.
QL458.4.B335   1997
595.4'4--dc20   96-19941
                                       CIP
                                       AC

Printed and bound in the United States of America

Acknowledgments
Illustrated by Tim Haywood
The publishers would like to thank the following for their permission to reproduce photographs: cover Jane
Burton/Bruce Coleman, title page J. A. L. Cooke/Oxford Scientific Films, 4 M. P. L. Fogden/Bruce Coleman, 5 top
Dr. Frieder Sauer/Bruce Coleman, 5 bottom Philip Sharpe/Oxford Scientific Films, 7 Scott Camazine/Oxford Scientific
Films, 10 Janos Jurka/Bruce Coleman, 11 Jane Burton/Bruce Coleman, 12 John McCammon/Oxford Scientific Films,
14 J. A. L. Cooke/Oxford Scientific Films, 15 top Mantis Wildlife Films/Oxford Scientific Films, 15 bottom Michael
Fogden/Oxford Scientific Films, 16 B. G. Murray, Jr./Animals Animals/Oxford Scientific Films, 18 top Mantis Wildlife
Films/Oxford Scientific Films, 18 bottom Scott Camazine/Oxford Scientific Films, 20 J. A. L. Cooke/Oxford Scientific
Films, 21 Gunter Zeisler/Bruce Coleman, 22 J. A. L. Cooke/Oxford Scientific Films, 24 Kim Taylor/Bruce Coleman,
25 top Carol Hughes/Bruce Coleman, 25 bottom Sean Morris/Oxford Scientific Films, 26 J. A. L. Cooke/Oxford
Scientific Films, 27 top Frieder Sauer/Bruce Coleman, 27 bottom Andy Purcell/Bruce Coleman, 28 Kim Taylor/Bruce
Coleman, 29 top Andy Purcell/Bruce Coleman, 29 bottom Mantis Wildlife Films/Oxford Scientific Films

*(Cover) A spider sits in the middle of her orb web. Instead of insects, all she has caught are
ragwort seeds that have blown in on the wind.*

CONTENTS

For almost 400 million years, spiders have been stalking their prey. Today, there are more than thirty thousand different kinds of spiders, and they are found in almost every part of the globe. They can survive in many environments, including hot deserts, polar regions, high mountains, dark caves, in houses and gardens, and even under water. They come in all sizes, from tiny moss-dwelling spiders only 0.017 inches (0.43 millimeters) across to giant bird-eating spiders with a leg span of over 11 inches (28 centimeters).

Spiders are hunters. Most prey on insects and other small animals such as centipedes and pill bugs. A few feed on larger prey, such as small snakes and lizards, frogs, and even small birds. Some spiders stalk or chase their prey; others lie in wait to ambush passing insects.

Bird-eating spiders are the largest spiders in the world, with bodies up to 3.5 inches (9 centimeters) long and a leg span of over 11 inches (28 centimeters).

A jumping spider lies in wait, then pounces on its prey. It has eyes all around its head for spotting prey; the large eyes in front help it judge distance and speed when jumping.

Let's explore how spiders build their webs, look at the many different webs and traps they spin, and examine how they use webs to catch their prey.

▶ *A golden orb weaver rests on its web below the remains of its last meal. The fine silk threads of the web are almost invisible — an effective trap for flying insects.*

Many use webs to trap their prey. Webs strung between leaves of branches catch flying insects, while other webs hidden on the ground or in crevices may entangle unwary passersby.

SPINNERS OF SILK

Spiders produce silk to make their webs. This silk is really a protein called fibroin. Spider silk is extremely strong — a length of silk would have to be over fifty miles (eighty kilometers) long before it would break under its own weight. It is also very elastic — more elastic than nylon. It can be stretched by almost one-third without snapping. This means that when some unfortunate creature blunders into a spider's web, the web stretches rather than breaks.

The silk is produced as a liquid by special glands inside the spider's abdomen. These glands are linked to tubelike organs called spinnerets,

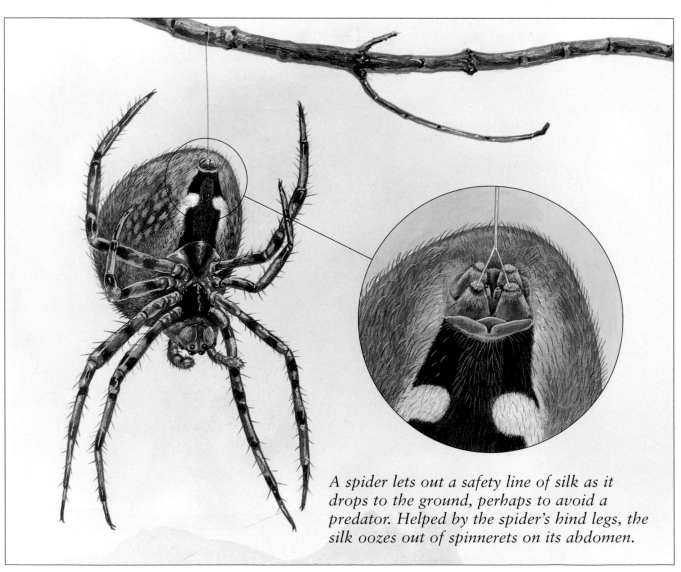

A spider lets out a safety line of silk as it drops to the ground, perhaps to avoid a predator. Helped by the spider's hind legs, the silk oozes out of spinnerets on its abdomen.

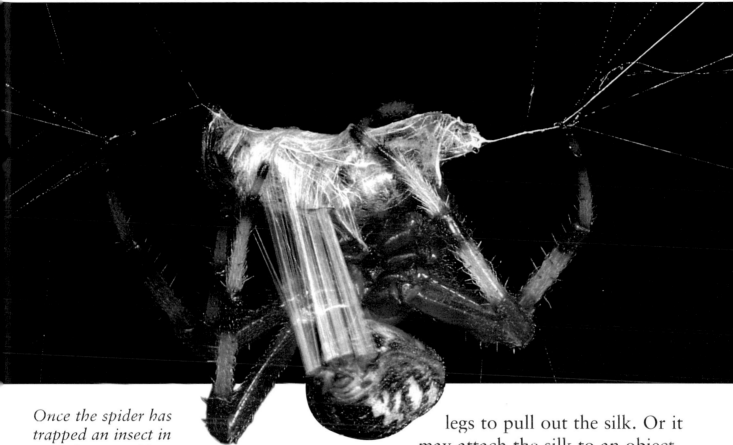

Once the spider has trapped an insect in its web, it quickly wraps its victim in thick bands of silk to prevent it from escaping or struggling and damaging the web.

which open to the outside through small nipples. The angle of the spinnerets is controlled by muscles and can be varied at will. Once the liquid silk is exposed to the air, it hardens into a thread.

The spider does not use muscles to force the silk out of its spinnerets. Instead, it uses the claws on its hind legs to pull out the silk. Or it may attach the silk to an object, then walk away from it. This pulling action exerts a tension on the silk that makes it solidify in a way that gives it strength.

A spider's silk glands may produce more than one kind of silk. Dry silk is used for drag lines and for cocoons to protect the spider's eggs, while sticky silk is used to catch food. Some spiders use their claws to fluff up the silk thread into a fuzzy mass that entangles the scales and hairs of their insect prey.

SHIMMERING ORBS

One of the most intricately constructed webs is the orb web, in which a spiral of silk is laid around a series of silk spokes that spread out from a central point. Orb weavers are found in most parts of the world. Some of their webs may be three feet (one meter) across — intended for large flying insects but big enough and strong enough to catch small birds.

▼ *1. To start an orb web, the spider must first make a bridge line between two high points. It may let loose a silk thread onto the breeze and hope it catches on a suitable object, or it may travel with the thread to the second anchor point. The bridge lines of some tropical orb weavers may be several feet long and may even span small rivers.*

▲ *2. Now the spider travels back along this first line, spinning a stronger thread, which it leaves dangling below it.*

▼ *3. The spider then returns to the middle of the line, grasps this thread, and drops to the ground or to a suitable twig or leaf. This forms the third anchor point.*

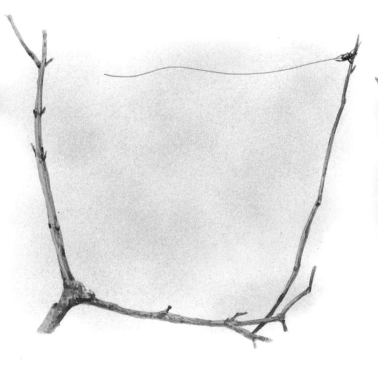

▶ 4. Next, the spider makes a series of extra framework threads around the outside and lays down the radial threads, working from the center outward, and anchoring them to the basic framework. So far, all the silk used has been dry, not sticky.

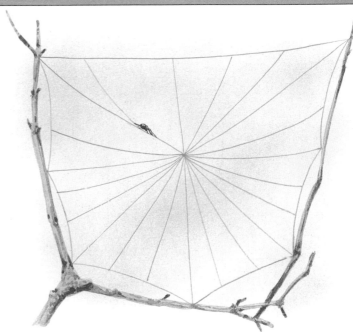

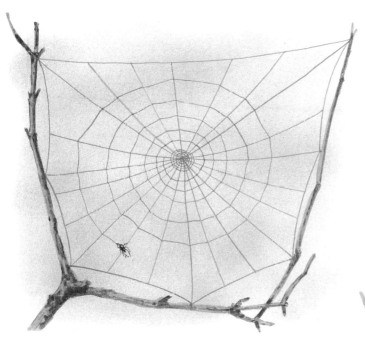

◀ 5. Still using dry silk, the spider now makes a tight spiral in the center of the web to anchor the radials and reinforce them. Further out, the spider makes a widely spaced temporary spiral, working outward from the inner part of the web. The gap between the outer spiral and the inner spiral will allow the spider to cross from one side of the web to the other later.

▶ 6. At last it is time to make the sticky catching spiral. Glue-covered threads of silk produced by a different set of silk glands are carefully attached to the radials to form a tight spiral. The spider works from the outside toward the hub, eating the silk from the temporary spiral as it goes. As the spider attaches the threads of the sticky spiral, it plucks them sharply with a claw. This causes the glue to break up into separate droplets.

THE TRAP IS COMPLETE

The whole web has been made in less than thirty minutes. The spider has added a reinforced platform so it can rest in the center of the web. Spiders usually retreat to the shelter of nearby leaves by day, out of sight of predators such as birds.

Spiders are very economical creatures. Their webs are made with the bare minimum of silk — silk is so strong that only very thin threads need be used. Any web that is damaged or not needed is eaten. Robust webs may survive for weeks or even months, but more delicate webs may be eaten and remade every night.

Like most spiders, orb weavers have eight eyes, but they do not rely on vision to detect prey. Instead, they use the vibrations of the web caused by the struggling creature. The spider rests on the platform in the web, or in a retreat, resting a leg on one of the silk threads. The slightest vibration of the web sends a signal along this thread. By testing the tension of the various threads, the spider can tell exactly where the prey is trapped. Small prey will be bitten immediately, but larger ones will be bound with silk first to prevent them from escaping.

A garden spider sits on the dry silk platform at the center of its web. Its feet rest on the silken spokes, waiting for the vibrations of struggling prey.

▲ *A garden spider dines on a crane fly. It injects it with digestive juices, then sucks up the resulting liquid.*

How does the spider manage to move about the web without sticking to the threads? An orb weaver holds its body well clear of the web. Its tiny claws can grasp the dry threads between the sticky ones. Its feet and legs also have an oily covering that prevents them being caught on the sticky threads.

Orb weavers have an extra claw on each foot and a series of barbed hairs that help them grasp the silk.

VARIATIONS ON A THEME

Hunted by birds, lizards, and other small vertebrates, spiders have their own enemies. Most spiders are active mainly at night. Many orb weavers remain in the hub of the web by day, their body color blending with their background. Others curl up leaves to make retreats at the side of their webs or build bits of dead leaf and twig into the hub to hide behind. The fine silk threads are transparent so the web is not easily seen unless it is decorated with dewdrops or crystals of frost. A few orb weavers vibrate the web so rapidly when disturbed that it becomes almost invisible.

The hubs of some webs are decorated with silk that has been fluffed out until it appears thick and white. This silk often forms zigzag patterns radiating from the web or spiraling around it. The purpose of these silk patterns is not clear. They may help to conceal the spider

or reflect the sun's rays. Perhaps they warn birds and larger flying insects that the web is there, thus avoiding unnecessary damage.

If danger threatens, the St. Andrew's cross spider vibrates its web violently so it is hard to see. The zigzagging bands may help strengthen the web for this.

▲ *The triangle spider holds the corner of the web itself so it can adjust the tension. When an insect lands in the web, the spider releases the slack silk of the anchor line so the web sags and further entangles the prey.*

The triangle spider makes a web that looks like a segment of an orb web. Another spider, *Pasilobus*, from New Guinea, makes a triangular web with sticky spiral threads that break when an insect flies into them. The spider then hauls its prey up.

Some spiders make horizontal orb webs. Sometimes, these are delicate temporary structures, but in some species, they are large and long lasting, held in place by guy lines to plants and twigs above and below the web.

LASSOING PREY

If you are exploring the Australian eucalyptus forests just before nightfall, you may easily pass by what looks like a small slender twig. It is a net-casting spider in its camouflage position. At dusk, the spider becomes active. Its huge eyes, adapted to nocturnal vision, have led to its popular name of "ogre-faced spider."

To prepare for the night's hunting, this spider spins a framework of silk threads about a foot (thirty centimeters) above the ground. Once darkness has fallen, the spider spins a simple oblong framework about the size of a postage stamp and anchors it to the vegetation with a few horizontal threads. Then, it spins a series of highly elastic zigzag threads, using a special organ called a cribellum, fluffing out the silk with combs of hairs on its vibrating hind feet. This is dry silk. It traps its victims not by sticking to them but by getting them entangled in its many tiny loops.

Once the net is complete, the spider stretches out its front legs to measure just the right height to hold the net. Then it dangles head-down from its

When at rest, the net-casting spider is almost invisible. It folds its legs to lie along the twig, and its large eyes are hidden under the fringes on its legs. At night, it turns into a fearsome hunter.

◀ The net-casting spider has the largest simple eyes of any invertebrate. There is only a short distance between the retina and the lens (the focal length), which improves their light-gathering. Each eye contains about ten thousand light receptors, each of which absorbs two thousand times more light than the receptors of spiders that hunt in daylight.

▶ The net-casting spider spins a hammock-shaped web to catch its prey. Hanging from a thread, it will wait for insects to pass below, then fling the net over them.

platform of threads, holding the net ready with its front two pairs of legs. As soon as its two huge front eyes spot a passing insect, it flings the net, stretching it to its full size. It lassoes the prey and pulls it off the ground.

Not all spiders rely on tiny beads of glue on sticky silk threads. Some produce much larger globules of glue and have very unusual ways of using them. The bolas spider of Australia spins a horizontal thread of silk from which to lure her prey. She then spins a vertical line of silk up to twenty-eight inches (seventy-one centimeters) long, coated with several large beads of glue about the size of pinheads. She places an even larger globule of glue at the end of the line to weigh it down.

The spider now gives off a smell similar to that of certain female moths. This scent attracts the male moths towards the spider. As a moth approaches, the spider keeps perfectly still, just producing more scent to lure the moth even closer. As soon as it is within reach, she lifts the trap line and starts to whirl it around her until the sticky globules trap the moth.

Similar globs of glue are used by some scaffold-web spiders. Their messy web is slung between twigs well above the ground. From the underside of the web dangle trap lines tipped with chains of glue globules and

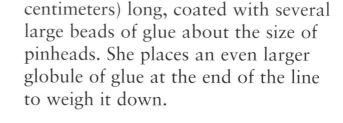

The bolas spider hunts at night when moths are flying. Luring moths within reach by giving off a scent like a female moth's, the spider twirls its glue-tipped line until it traps a moth.

anchored to the ground. Insects trying to move between these lines become stuck to the glue. As a result of their struggles, the trap lines break free from the ground. As they struggle, they become stuck to more and more trap lines. These lines are elastic, and the insect is jerked off its feet. The

A scaffold-web spider emerges from its retreat, alerted by the struggles of an insect trapped in the tangle of glue-tipped trap lines beneath its web.

spider then pulls it up to eat it. The silk of some of these webs is strong enough to hold a small lizard or even a mouse.

SHEETS AND BASKETS

Not all spider webs are as orderly as the orb webs. Even apparently messy tangles of silk can be highly effective traps. Insects, and even other spiders, may be trapped in the tangle of silk just long enough for the spider to rush out and bite them.

Many spiders do quite well using dry silk rather than sticky silk. The cribellate spiders have a special organ, the cribellum, that fluffs up the silk so the tiny feet of insects become tangled up in it. These spiders often produce lacy-looking sheet webs over the ground, on windowsills, or even on windowpanes.

Others use ordinary dry silk but weave an intricate net of threads to trip walking and hopping insects. These lattice webs may form flat sheets on solid surfaces, or they may be suspended and pulled into shape by a scaffold of other threads, forming hammocks, funnels, and domes, often with a funnel at the side where the spider lies in wait. In temperate regions in the early morning, grassy fields may be studded with thousands of tiny hammock webs

The tangled threads of tiny webs trip up insects crawling over the foliage so they fall into the hammocks below. (Inset) A close-up view of the fluffed-up silk produced by cribellate spiders.

glistening with dewdrops. Indoors, the sheetlike lattice webs of house spiders are an all too common sight in the houses of Europe and North America.

Sometimes, whole colonies of spiders form huge towers of hammock webs many feet high in the undergrowth of forests, especially in the tropics.

The network of threads above this hammock web isn't sticky, but it entangles crawling insects and flying insects, which drop into the hammock.

Insects blundering into the scaffolding fall into one of the many hammocks below. These webs often last for months; the damage caused by prey is easily repaired.

TUNNELS AND TRAPDOORS

One of the most ancient groups of spider are the mygalomorphs, which include some of the largest and most poisonous spiders in the world. Most of them live in permanent burrows, or in crevices or holes in timber, walls, or rocks. Underground burrows are lined with silk, while crevice-dwelling mygalomorphs usually live in silken "socks" or "purses." These spiders are fierce predators that ambush their prey.

The trap-door spiders of Australia live in burrows up to three feet (one meter) deep. In some species, the burrow is closed by a trap door made of dirt bound together by silk and attached by a silken hinge. Bits of twig, leaves, and other debris may be fixed to the surface of the door for added camouflage. The spider lurks in its burrow with the lid raised just enough for it to spot any prey that comes within reach.

Some of these spiders prepare a series of trip lines radiating from the burrow entrance. The spider waits inside,

A trapdoor spider waits at the entrance to its burrow, ready to pounce on passing insects.

resting its feet on the trip lines. As soon as an insect touches one of these, the spider opens its door and pounces.

Among the most poisonous of the mygalomorphs are the funnel-web spiders of Australia. These live in silken tubes, ending in a purselike

A funnel-web spider's powerful jaws often crush a victim to death before its poison has time to take effect.

chamber where the spider hides by day. At night, the spider lies in wait at the entrance, ready to strike. The bite from some funnel-web spiders is powerful enough to kill a human.

SILKEN PURSES AND DIVING BELLS

The water spider has found a novel use for a silken purse. This spider lives underwater in a silken "diving bell" filled with air, where it lies in wait for passing water insects and shrimps.

This spider starts by spinning a small silk platform, which it fixes to underwater plants. Then it returns to the surface and somehow manages to trap a bubble of air between the hairs on its abdomen and its hind legs. The spider releases this air directly under the platform so that it floats up and is trapped by the silk. It then enlarges the edges of the bell before bringing back more and more air bubbles, until it has built a bell-shaped home full of air.

The spider lies in wait at the entrance of the bell and is quick to sense vibrations in the water that tell of the approach of prey. Once the spider has seized its prey, it drags it back to the bell. It must feed here, or the digestive juices it exudes over its meal would be diluted by the water.

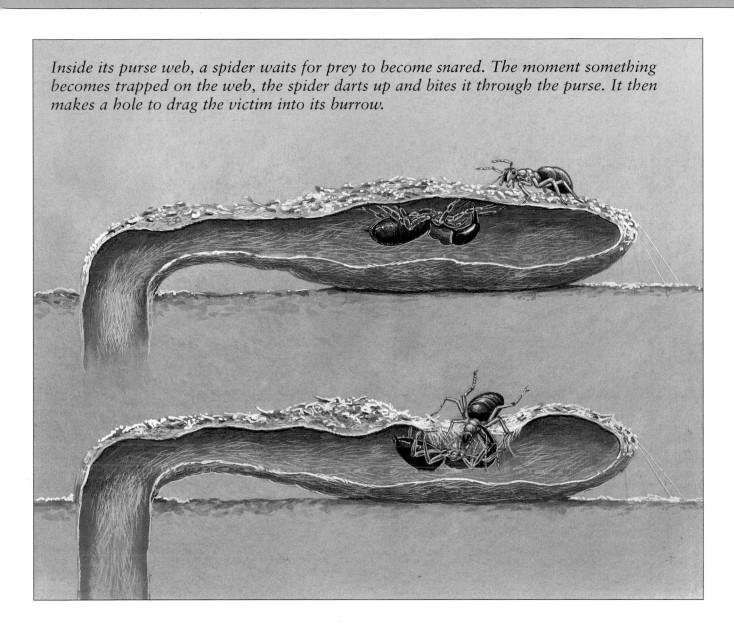

Inside its purse web, a spider waits for prey to become snared. The moment something becomes trapped on the web, the spider darts up and bites it through the purse. It then makes a hole to drag the victim into its burrow.

In the northern hemisphere live smaller relatives of the funnel-web spiders, the purse-web spiders. A purse-web spider lives in a burrow lined with silk. A purselike extension of this silken tube lies on the ground. When covered with pieces of bark, dead leaves, and other debris, it is very hard to see. The spider waits for dinner here, where it can sink its fangs into any creature walking above its head. The web also serves as a nursery for the spider's young. Some North American purse-web spiders extend the silk tube up the trunk of a tree to trap insects crawling on the bark.

DRAG LINES AND DATING

Spiders have many different uses for silk besides spinning webs. One of the most common is to use a silk thread as a safety line. When threatened, a spider may drop suddenly to the ground, but it usually gives out a silken safety line (drag line) as it does so.

sending out silk behind them. They can drift for vast distances before coming down to earth again. Some may even have colonized islands by drifting from the mainland in this way. The early morning dew often shows up the many tiny drag lines left by ballooning spiders.

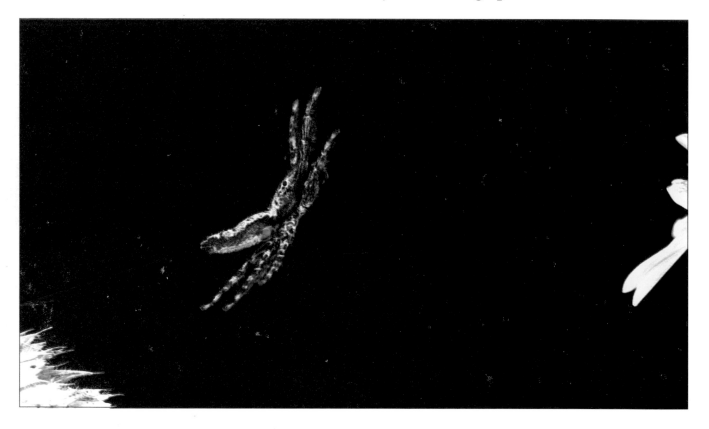

Jumping spiders, which often make huge leaps onto their prey, send out safety lines in case they have misjudged their jump.

Spiders also use silk to help them colonize new areas. Very small spiders, including the young of many species, will take off into the breeze,

Spiders also use silk for signaling. Male spiders are usually quite a lot smaller than the females, and when they go looking for a mate, they are seriously at risk of being eaten by a potential partner. One way to avoid this is to vibrate her web in a

A male orb-weaver spider caresses his much larger mate. He is so much smaller than her that he is quite unable to defend himself if she decides to eat him.

particular way that signals that he is courting — and not her dinner. Similar signals are used by certain spiders that live in vast communal webs stretching often for hundreds of feet along

◄ *When spiders molt their skins, they are at risk for several hours while the new skin underneath hardens in the air. If they are dangling from a fine thread, they are less obvious, and it's harder for an enemy to reach them.*

hedgerows. Young spiders are recognized as members of the family by the vibrations they produce as they travel over the web. Communal webs give youngsters a good chance of survival, as they have a plentiful supply of food until they have learned to catch it for themselves.

NURSERY WEBS

Many female spiders spin cocoons in which to protect their eggs. Cocoon silk is made in special glands. The eggs are produced in a sticky fluid that binds them together, then encased in fluffy silk. The cocoon prevents the eggs drying out and helps protect against attack by parasitic wasps and other predators. Cocoons also provide a warm safe place for eggs to survive over the winter.

The cocoons are often guarded by the female spider until the eggs hatch. Then the spiderlings are left to fend for themselves. Indeed, many spiders die soon after producing their cocoons. Some spiders, such as the huntsman spiders, produce smooth hard cocoons, which they carry in their mouths or fixed to their spinnerets.

The nursery-web spider also carries her cocoon with her. In cold weather, she may lean back and expose the eggs to the sun to warm them. Just before the eggs hatch, the spider spins a tentlike web, the "nursery web," and

A golden orb-weaver spins a fluffy cocoon of golden silk to cover her mass of pink eggs.

26

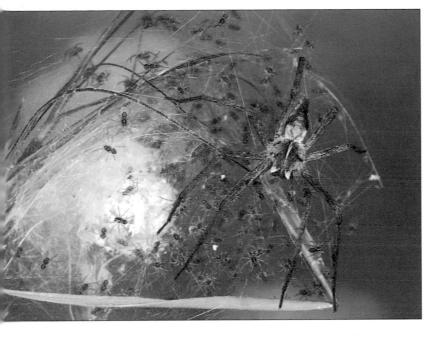

A nursery-web spider guards the spiderlings that have just hatched from the white cocoon in the middle of the "nursery web."

Cocoons are often covered with pieces of bark, leaves, and other debris. A few spiders produce cocoons that look rather like bird or mammal droppings. Leaf-curling spiders roll up leaves and hide their eggs inside, fixing the rolled leaf in position with strong sticky silk.

suspends the sac inside it. The newly hatched spiderlings will stay here until their first molt.

▼ *The fishing spider* Dolomedes *carries such a large egg sac that she has to walk on tiptoe. From time to time, she dips the sac in water to keep the eggs moist.*

OTHER SILK SPINNERS

Spiders are not the only animals to produce silk. The most famous are the silkworms — the caterpillars of the silk moths — which produce cocoons of silk. Their silk is used to make fine fabrics and embroidery thread. Silkworms have spinnerets on their heads. As in spiders, the silk is exuded as a liquid, which hardens into a thread on contact with the air. This silk is not so fine as spider silk, and the whole cocoon is made of a single thread up to three thousand feet (nine hundred meters) long. After suitable treatment, this can be spooled off the cocoon as a single thread.

Caddis flies are mothlike insects with brownish papery wings that live along the banks of rivers and ponds. Their larvae live under water in protective cases made from pieces of plant material, stones, twigs, or even snail shells. The larva glues these materials together using silk, which is spun from the mouth. The head and front legs protrude from the case, allowing the larva to crawl around.

Each caddis species produces its own kind of case. Some cut lengths of underwater plants and arrange them in a spiral

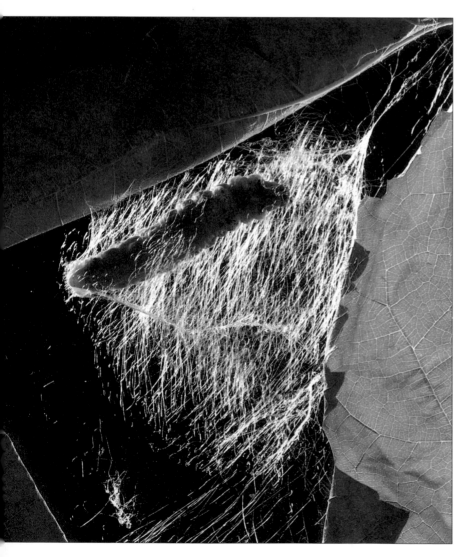

A silkworm larva spins the cocoon in which it will change into a silk moth. The whole structure is made from a single very long thread. When it is finished, the caterpillar inside will be invisible.

This caddis fly larva lives in a case made of shells glued together with silk. As the caddis grows, it will add more shells to hide and protect its body.

band to form a cone-shaped case. Others, especially in fast-flowing streams, make cases of pebbles that help to weigh them down.

▼ *Weaver ants live in nests inside balls of leaves woven together with silk. The silk is produced by the ants' larvae. The ants use them like tubes of glue, ensuring that the silk is stuck to just the right point on the leaf.*

The larvae can be persuaded to use all sorts of materials if robbed of their usual homes; glass beads make particularly pretty cases.

Although all these insects produce silk, spiders are the only animals that regularly produce silk as adults. Silk plays a major part in their lifestyles — in homes and hunting traps, and to immobilize their prey, protect their eggs, and signal to potential mates. Truly, they are the wizards of webs.

cocoon: a structure protecting eggs or larvae from predators or bad weather.

invertebrate: an animal without a backbone. Insects, spiders, snails, and worms are all invertebrates.

lens: the part of the eye that focuses the light onto the retina.

predator: an animal that hunts and eats other animals.

prey: an animal that is hunted and eaten by another animal.

radial thread: a thread that forms one of the spokes of an orb web.

retina: a layer of light-sensitive cells at the back of the eye. These cells send nerve signals to the brain to tell it about the light coming into the eye.

trap line: a sticky thread that hangs down from a spider's web to trap insects and other prey.

vertebrate: an animal with a backbone. Fish, frogs, lizards, birds, cats, and humans are all vertebrates.

FURTHER READING

Back, Christine, and Barrie Watts. *Spider's Web*. Morristown, NJ: Silver Burdett, 1986.

Bailey, Donna. *Spiders*. Chatham, NJ: Raintree Steck-Vaughn Publications, 1992.

Craig, Janet. *Amazing World of Spiders*. Mahwah, NJ: Troll Associates, 1990.

Dallinger, Jane. *Spiders*. Minneapolis: Lerner, 1981.

Lovett, Sarah. *Extremely Weird Spiders*. Santa Fe, NM: John Muir Publications, 1991.

Morris, Dean. *Spiders*. Chatham, NJ: Raintree Steck-Vaughn Publications, 1987.

Murray, Peter. *Spiders*. Plymouth, MN: Child's World, 1992.

Parsons, Alexandra. *Amazing Spiders*. New York: Alfred A. Knopf, 1990.

Preston-Mafham, Rod, and Ken Preston-Mafham. *Spiders of the World*. New York: Facts on File, 1984.

Schnieper, Claudia. *Amazing Spiders*. Minneapolis: Carolrhoda Books, 1989.

INDEX

Numbers in *italic* indicate pictures